Maria Gruber

Tyrolean
Specialties

KOMPASS **Kitchen Delights**

Before You Begin!

Anyone who visits Tyrol is delighted by the hearty dishes and the diversity of Tyrolean recipes.

For centuries, Tyrol's neighboring countries and down-home farm dishes have shaped Tyrolean food to a considerable extent. The once meager meals eaten by the farmers and peasants were based on a foundation of grains and dairy products. Meats only rarely found their way to the table, and even then, mostly on religious holidays like Christmas and Easter. Today, a wide range of specialties are still associated with Tyrol and have their roots in the everyday farm life. There are also a number of dishes which people enjoy cooking and eating again and again.

In this book, you will find a variety of popular entrées and snacks, next to delicate and more hearty soups. Tyrolean dumpling recipes are also an integral part of this book, as are the well-known pastries and baked goods. The last chapter is devoted to deep-fried pastries and other baked specialties.

Tyrol is also well-known for its breads. I therefore compiled a short chapter covering some lovely bread recipes, as well as a whole series of tips on baking and dough preparation. This is followed by a chapter that briefly describes the most typical Tyrolean dishes. Finally, you will find a glossary of cooking and baking terms.

You will certainly learn

about these different dishes quickly and have fun trying your hand at them. I wish you the very best and, as always, much success.

Yours,
Maria Gruber

Table of Contents

Tyrolean Specialties - A Brief Overview

Tyrolean cuisine goes far beyond the ever-popular Bacon Dumpling and Tyrolean Gröstl, the two dishes that most quickly come to mind. Nevertheless, the hearty Tyrolean food was originally quite plain farmer's sustenance. In the morning, there was often only a simple "Brennsuppe" (roux soup) or a one-skillet meal. At noon the peasants would eat dumplings of one sort or another. For the afternoon meal ("Marend"), milk with peasant bread, and then at night, a single-skillet meal or thick soup.

The main vegetables available were cabbage, beets and green beans, along with potatoes, which were prepared in a variety of ways. Meat was rarely eaten. Fresh meat needed to be preserved immediately. Pickling and treating meat in a liquid consisting of wine and water, and then smoking it was the only way to preserve meats in the early days. Even today, the highly prized **Tyrolean bacon** is made in the same way.

Tyrolean bacon is a key ingredient in many of the recipes, or can also be used to round the taste, for example in the appetizing **Bacon Dumplings** and **Tyrolean Gröstl**, a dish of sliced, cooked potatoes and pork. Tyrolean cuisine, in addition to these traditional peasant dishes of its origin, offers a variety of other delicious meals that are essentials on any Tyrolean menu. From the merchants' homes, we have a recipe for **Tyrolean Liver**. Typical soups are **Sour Soup** and hearty **Barley Soup**, which is prepared with pearl barley and smoked pork. In addition, there is an entire spectrum of dumplings made of noodle or potato

dough. One particularly filling dish is **Cheese Spaetzle**. Deep-fried dough specialties also play a key role in Tyrolean cuisine, in particular **Strauben**. During the Advent season before Christmas, **Zelten**, or fruit bread, is made of dried plums, dried pears, dried figs, and plump raisins, as well as a variety of nuts. After a hearty meal or to accompany a filling "Jause" (pronounced "Yow-zeh") or afternoon snack, many Tyroleans enjoy a **schnaps**. In Tyrol, the traditional "Obstler" (fruit brandy) is quite popular, along with more special drinks such as "Enzian," a clear brandy flavored with gentian root.

REPUBLIK ÖSTERREICH

VORARLBERG

WIEN

Bregenz

Vorarl-
berg

Innsbruck

T i r o l (Tyrol)

S a l z b

S

Osttirol

Lienz

BURGENLAND

KÄRNTEN

NIEDERÖSTERREICH

OB

Ober- •Linz

erreich

oper Austria)

Nieder-
österreich

•St. Pölten

(Lower Austria)

WIEN
(Vienna)

•Eisenstadt

Burgen-

land

Steiermark

(Styria)

•Graz

ärnten

(arinthia)

•Klagenfurt

0   50 km

ICH   SALZBURG   STEIERMARK   TIROL

Essential Kitchen Terms

Douse
To quickly add hot liquid to frying meat or vegetables, for instance, to loosen pan drippings

Rinse
To rinse boiled foods, such as spaetzle, with cold water to prevent sticking and halt the cooking process

Drain
To place food in a colander or sieve and let drip off

Roll Out
To roll out dough

Roux
Butter and flour mixture, heated slowly

Grind
To pass meat through a grinder

Let Rise
To place a yeast dough in a bowl, cover with a dry dishtowel, and let stand in a warm place, until it has almost doubled in size

Bind
To bind a fluid with egg yolk, cream or butter

Mill
To press through a fine sieve or use a blender to finely purée potatoes

Grate
To grate coarsely

Let Rest
To let specific doughs stand and "rest"

Reduce
To boil until thickened; sauces or pan drippings are thickened by evaporation to bring out their flavors more intensely

Beat
To beat ingredients into a foamy consistency using an egg-beater

Fold
To carefully mix beaten egg whites and batter. The best way to do this is using a spatula, lifting the batter over the egg whites and gently mixing until well combined.

Beat
To briefly beat egg

Simmer
To allow delicate dishes to continue cooking below the boiling point

Tyrolean Bacon Dumpling Soup / Speckknödelsuppe

3-4 stale hard rolls or Kaiser rolls	5 oz. lean Tyrolean bacon
2 cups warm milk	3 eggs, ½ cup flour
1 T parsley	5 cups hearty beef broth
1 small onion, salt	2 T chopped chives

● Cut stale rolls into cubes, place in mixing bowl. Finely dice bacon and add to bread cubes. Sprinkle with chopped parsley. Mix eggs and milk and pour over bread/bacon mixture. Stir and let stand for 20 minutes. Peel and finely chop onions. Sauté in butter until translucent.

● Add sautéed onions and flour to bread mixture. Add salt and mix well.

● Form small dumplings and let simmer in salted, gently boiling water for approx. 15 minutes.

● Serve in beef broth. Garnish with chopped chives.

Tyrolean Beef Broth with Bacon Squares / Speckschöberlsuppe

1 ½ oz Tyrolean smoked bacon	2 - 3 T milk
5 T soft butter	½ cup flour
3 egg yolks	3 egg whites
salt, pepper, ground nutmeg	4 cups hearty, hot beef broth
	2 T chopped chives

- Preheat oven to 400° F.

- Finely dice bacon and fry in a skillet. Let cool. Combine egg yolks and butter in a small bowl and beat until very light in color. Add salt, pepper and nutmeg. Stir in milk and flour. Continue stirring until creamy. Stir in bacon.

- In a separate bowl, beat egg whites until stiff. Gently fold into dough mixture.

- Spread dough evenly onto a greased baking sheet.

- Bake in a 400° F oven until golden brown. Let cool somewhat. Cut into squares or diamonds. Ladle soup into bowls, place squares or diamond bacon bits in soup, sprinkle with chopped chives and serve immediately.

Tripe Soup / Saure Suppe

1 lb boiled tripe (beef or pork)	salt, pepper and ground allspice
2 onions	2 cloves garlic, crushed
2 T butter	grated rind of 1 lemon
1 - 2 T flour	1 bay leaf
4 cups hearty beef broth	dash of white wine or vinegar

● Cut tripe into fine strips. Peel and chop onions. Melt butter in a large soup pot, add onions and sauté until translucent. Add tripe strips and fry with onions. Sprinkle with flour and continue frying until golden-brown. Add hot beef broth.

● Season with salt, pepper, ground allspice, crushed garlic, grated lemon rind, and bay leaf.

● Simmer for 30 - 45 minutes. Just before serving, add dash of white wine or vinegar to taste.

Alpbach Beer Soup / Alpbacher Biersuppe

2 T butter	¼ cup sugar
2 T flour	approx. 2 cups strong beer
approx. ¼ cup milk	1 egg
1-2 cloves	pepper
1 tsp ground cinnamon	salt
grated rind of ½ lemon	2 - 3 T sour cream

● Melt butter in a large pot. Sprinkle with flour to make a light roux. Add milk and simmer while stirring for approx. 10 minutes.

● Add cloves, cinnamon, grated lemon rind, and sugar to the roux.

● Bring to a boil again and add beer. Heat gently but do not allow to boil. Strain mixture through a fine sieve.

● Beat egg. Add to soup as a binder, stirring constantly. Season strongly. Add sour cream if desired and serve immediately.

East Tyrolean Barley Soup / Osttiroler Gerstensuppe

● Rinse pearl barley with cold water. Soak in cold water overnight. Finely dice the bacon and slowly brown in a large skillet or pot. Drain pearl barley, add to pot and fry with the browned bacon.
Add part of the broth and simmer.

● Peel and finely dice the onions. Wash, peel and julienne cut carrots, celery root and leek. Add vegetables and onions to the bacon/barley mixture and add remaining broth. Add salt and pepper to taste. Bring to a boil, then reduce heat. Simmer for approximately two hours,

| 3 oz barley |
| 5 oz bacon |
| 6 cups (2 ½ pts) beef stock |
| 2 small onions |
| 2 carrots |
| 1 large leek |
| 2 medium potatoes |
| salt |
| white pepper |
| pinch of nutmeg |
| 1 T flour |
| cold water |
| 2 T sour cream |
| 4 thin slices of crisp bacon |

or until barley is tender.

● One-half hour before serving, add finely diced potatoes to the soup. Slowly brown bacon strips until crisp. Ten minutes prior to serving, mix flour with cold water in a cup and add to soup to thicken. Correct the seasoning, add grated nutmeg and stir in sour cream. Do not boil soup after adding cream.

Garnish soup with crisp bacon strips when serving.

Serve with dark rye bread.

F.Y.I.

Barley soup is very popular among the entire mountain-dwelling populace of Austria, since barley grows well even at high altitudes (1500 m - 1700 m). Made without meat it was a favorite at Lent, served with onions browned in butter.

Tyrolean Potato Soup /
Tiroler Erdäpfelsuppe

2 carrots	ground caraway
1 - 2 stalks of celery	1 bay leaf
1 small parsley root	approx. 2 cups water
2 onions	4 cups beef broth
2 - 3 T butter	1 - 2 T flour
1 lb potatoes	¼ cup cold water
salt, marjoram, several black peppercorns	fresh parsley or chives, chopped

● Peel and dice carrots, celery, parsley root, onions, and potatoes. In a large soup pot, first sauté vegetables in butter, then add potatoes. Add salt, caraway, marjoram, peppercorns, and bay leaf. Add water and simmer until vegetables are tender.

● Stir occasionally and, if necessary, add more water.

● Simmer for approx. 45 minutes. When potatoes are tender, strain soup through a course sieve. Add beef broth. Make a thin paste of flour and cold water. Add to soup to bind. Bring soup to a boil and season to taste.

● Serve sprinkled with chopped parsley or chives.

Tyrolean Fish Gröstl / Stockfischgröstl

2 lbs dried cod	1 onion, finely diced
1 lb firm potatoes	salt, pepper
6 T butter, water	½ cup sour cream
1 clove garlic	1 T chopped parsley

● Soak dried cod in water overnight. Boil unpeeled potatoes until tender. Peel while still warm and slice.

● Remove fish from water, drain and place in boiling, slightly salted water for 10 - 15 minutes. Drain in a colander, remove bones and cut into small pieces.

● Melt butter in large skillet and sauté diced onions until translucent. Add sliced potatoes. Season with salt, pepper and crushed garlic.

● Add fish and continue to brown mixture. Remove from heat and add sour cream carefully. Sprinkle with chopped parsley and serve.

Our tip:
"Stockfischgröstl," a typical Tyrolean dish, is generally accompanied by Sauerkraut with Bacon ("Speckkraut"). The recipe is given on page 34.

Pork Roast Country Style /
Schweinsbraten nach Bauernart

3 lbs pork roast (leg)	oil
salt, pepper	1 - 2 cups of hot beef broth or water
1 clove garlic	
1 tsp whole caraway seeds	1 - 2 T flour, water
1 tsp thyme	sour cream to taste

● Preheat oven to 350° F. Rinse roast under cool water and pat dry with paper towel. Score fat layer in a diamond pattern with a sharp knife.

● Mix salt, pepper, crushed garlic, caraway, and thyme with a bit of oil.

Rub into roast, covering all sides.

● Place seasoned roast in a large roasting pan. Add hot broth or water to pan. Bake for 2 - 2 ½ hours, basting occasionally.

● To prepare gravy, remove

roast from pan and pour drippings into a small saucepan. Stir flour into ½ cup of cold water and add to drippings. Bring to a boil. If desired, add sour cream for a richer sauce.

Serve with bread dumplings, or potatoes and carrots roasted with the pork, or sauerkraut.

Tyrolean-Style Liver / Leber Tiroler Art

1 lb pork or veal liver	1 T flour
3 oz Tyrolean bacon	½ cup hot beef broth
1 onion	dry white wine
¼ cup butter	salt
pepper	

● Rinse liver with cold water and pat dry with paper towel. Cut liver and bacon into thin slices. Peel and finely dice onion.

● Melt butter in a large skillet. Sauté onion until translucent. Add bacon slices and continue frying.

● Then add slices of liver. Season with pepper. Dust with flour and continue to fry, stirring constantly. Douse with hot broth, add a dash of dry white wine. Salt to taste and stir.

● Bring to a boil and serve immediately.

Serve with pan-roasted potatoes and green salad.

Tyrolean Goulash / Tiroler Saftgulasch

5 oz Tyrolean bacon	½ cup hot beef broth or hot water
¼ cup butter	1 tsp caraway seeds
½ lb onions	1 tsp marjoram
1 T sweet paprika	salt
1 lb beef (cut into 1-inch cubes)	pepper
1 clove garlic	

● Finely dice bacon and sauté in butter. Add peeled and finely diced onion. Sprinkle with paprika.

● Continue to stir constantly over high heat. Add beef cubes and stir until beef is browned on all sides.

● Add broth or water. Season with caraway, marjoram, salt, and pepper. Cover and simmer for 1 - 1 ½ hours.

● Stir occasionally, adding water if necessary.

● Goulash is ready when meat is tender and onions have dissolved in the sauce.

Serve with bread dumplings. If desired, goulash can also be served with sliced frankfurters and fried egg (see photo).

F.Y.I.
Tyrolean Goulash is also very good with "Polenta" (recipe on p. 36). Served with a soft side dish, Tyrolean Goulash was the traditional Sunday meal of the Tyrolean farmer.

Tyrolean Farmer's Feast / Bauernschmaus

4 - 6 slices of smoked ham	juniper berries
salt	4 frankfurters
ground caraway	4 slices of roast pork
shortening	(from shoulder or
2 oz Tyrolean bacon	pork butt)
1 small onion	bacon dumplings (see p. 9)
1 lb sauerkraut	pickles

● Rinse smoked ham slices in cold water. Pat dry with paper towel, season and brown in melted shortening. Keep warm over low burner.

● Dice bacon and fry in a large pot. Peel and finely dice onion; add to bacon. Then add sauerkraut, season with caraway and juniper berries, cover and simmer until tender.

● Make two crossed slices in the end of each frankfurter. Place on top of sauerkraut to heat. Prepare Bacon Dumplings (see p. 9).

● On a large platter, first place sauerkraut and dumplings, and then arrange meats. Garnish with pickles.

Tyrolean Beef Pot Roast / Rindsbraten

3 lbs beef roast (shoulder)	½ cup dry red wine
4 oz Tyrolean bacon	2 cups beef broth
salt, pepper	1 carrot
½ tsp each of caraway seed and marjoram	1 parsley root
2 small onions	¼ celery root
1 clove garlic	1 small leek
5 - 6 T shortening or butter	½ lb potatoes

● Rinse meat under cold running water and pat dry with paper towel. Cut bacon into thin slices and lard roast. Season with salt, pepper, caraway and marjoram.

● Peel and finely chop onions and garlic. Briefly sauté in melted shortening or butter. Add roast and brown on all sides.

● Douse with broth and red wine. Cover and simmer until tender over low flame.

● After about 1 hour, add finely diced carrot, parsley and celery root, as well as peeled and diced potatoes. Total roasting time: 1 ½ - 1 ¾ hours.

● Remove roast from pot, slice and serve. Serve vegetables separately.

Serve with dumplings.

Roast Veal Knuckle / Kalbsstelze

1 large veal knuckle (approx. 3 lbs)	1 - 2 garlic cloves
salt, pepper	2 ½ T butter or shortening

● Briefly rinse veal knuckle under cold water and pat dry with paper towel. Season on all sides and rub with peeled, pressed cloves of garlic.

● Melt butter or shortening in a large roasting pan and brown meat on all sides.

● Roast in a 350° F oven for 1 ½ to 2 hours. Turn occasionally and baste frequently.

● Serve veal knuckle as a whole or slice, returning meat to bone after cutting. Arrange on a pre-warmed platter.

Serve with boiled potatoes and vegetables.

Stuffed Veal Roast / Gefüllter Kalbsbraten

3 lbs veal roast, sliced to make flat layer of meat	2 T chopped parsley
salt	ground paprika (sweet)
pepper	2 egg yolks
3 onions	4 - 5 T cream
1 clove garlic	6 T butter or shortening
1 small green pepper	½ cup dry white wine
½ lb very lean Tyrolean bacon or smoked ham	1 cup beef broth
	1 carrot
	cream

● Briefly rinse meat under cold water and pat dry with a paper towel. Lay flat and season with salt and pepper.

● Peel and finely chop

onions and garlic. Cut green pepper in half, remove core and seeds, and cut into coarse squares. Mix these ingredients with finely diced bacon or ham, chopped parsley, paprika, egg yolks and cream. Purée in a food processor to make a paste.

● Spread paste on meat, leaving a border free all the way around. Roll meat up like a jelly roll and fasten with toothpicks or kitchen twine.

● Heat butter or shortening in a roasting pan, brown roast on all sides and place in a 300° F oven. Roast for approx. 2 hours. Occasionally baste with white wine or beef broth.

● Approximately 30 minutes before removing roast from oven, place finely chopped onions and carrot in the roaster. Remove roast from roaster and place on a platter. Strain drippings into a sauce pan, heat briefly and add cream.

Serve with semolina dumplings and green salad.

Tyrolean Pan-Fried Potatoes / Tiroler G'röstl

approx. 1 ½ lbs potatoes, cooked	white pepper
1 large onion	1 tsp marjoram
12 oz roast pork	2 - 3 T parsley, coarsely chopped
5 oz smoked sausage or ham	4 eggs
3 oz shortening or 4 T oil	butter or margarine (for frying)
salt	

● Peel boiled potatoes and slice (leftover boiled potatoes also work well). Peel and finely chop onions. Cut pork roast and sausage into thin, bite-sized slices.

● Heat shortening in a skillet and sauté onions until translucent. Stir in potatoes and meat; fry, turning ingredients occasionally. Reduce heat and fry for 10-15 min. more. Season with salt, pepper and marjoram.

● Chop parsley and sprinkle over potatoes when serving. Often served with a fried egg.

Our tip:
Tyrolean G'röstl goes well with Austrian-style cole slaw, which is made with hot bacon dressing.

F.Y.I.
Genuine Tyrolean G'röstl is made with roast pork. If you use leftover beef, you then have "Farmer's G'röstl." Add sautéed veal to the potatoes and you have "Innsbruck-style G'röstl," also known as "Gentleman's G'röstl." Use approx. 1 lb meat and somewhat less potatoes when making the latter.

Roast Chicken / Brathendl

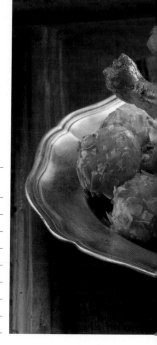

2 lbs chicken (fresh or frozen and thawed)
salt
pepper
¼ cup melted butter
1 small onion
1 large carrot
1 cup hot chicken broth
½ tsp paprika
1 T chopped parsley

● Preheat oven to 350° F. Rinse chicken well under cold water and pat dry with paper towel. Season inside and out with salt and pepper. Truss wings to back and tie legs together.

● Place chicken, breast-side down, in a roasting pan. Baste with most of melted butter. Add peeled and coarsely chopped onions and carrot to the pan. Place in oven.

● Turn chicken after about 30 minutes. Baste with chicken broth and reduce oven temperature to 300° F. Mix remaining butter with paprika powder and spread on breast of chicken. Return to oven. Total roasting time is about 1 hour.

● Remove chicken from oven, place on pre-warmed platter and sprinkle with chopped parsley. Strain drippings and serve separately.

Serve with dumplings and green salad.

Chicken in Horseradish Sauce / Huhn in Krensoße

1 fresh chicken, approx. 2 - 3 lbs	3 oz ground almonds
salt, pepper, one onion	¼ cup flour
2 cups chicken broth	4 ½ T butter
3 oz freshly grated horseradish	½ cup cream
	ground ginger to taste

● Rinse chicken in cold water, pat dry with paper towel, and cut into pieces. Season, place in deep skillet, and cover with chicken broth. If necessary, add more water to cover chicken pieces completely. Spread with horseradish, almonds and chopped onions. Bring to a boil, cover and simmer for approx. 50 - 60 minutes.

● Remove meat from pan. Place on deep platter and keep warm. Make a paste of butter and flour. Add to sauce, heating until thickened, stirring constantly. Stir in cream. Sprinkle in ginger to taste. Pour sauce over chicken pieces and serve.

Serve with boiled potatoes or rice.

Tyrolean Venison with Wild Mushrooms / Unterländer Wildfleisch mit Schwammerln

1 ¼ lbs venison	pepper
3 - 4 T oil	1 bay leaf
2 onions, 2 cloves	dash of apple cider vinegar
2 cups dry red wine	¼ lb fresh wild mushrooms
salt	butter, cream, cranberries

● Rinse meat briefly under cold water. Pat dry with paper towel and cut into cubes. Heat oil in large skillet and brown meat, stirring constantly. Add chopped onions. Douse with red wine.

● Season and add dash of vinegar. Bring to a boil and then simmer for 45 - 60 minutes until tender.

● Clean, wash and cut mushrooms into quarters. Add to pan 10 minutes before end of cooking time, and simmer with meat. Add butter and cream to taste. Serve garnished with cranberries.

Serve with noodles, red cabbage with chestnuts.

Red Cabbage with Chestnuts / Kastanienblaukraut

1 head red cabbage (approx. 2 lbs)	1 small bay leaf
¼ cup butter or shortening	approx. 1 cup water or beef broth
2 T sugar	2 T vinegar
1 onion	1 apple, 4 T red wine
salt	1 T flour
ground caraway	10 chestnuts (pre-cooked)

● Finely shred cabbage. Rinse under running water and let drip well. In a large pot, brown sugar and finely chopped onion in hot butter or shortening. Add cabbage, spices, water and/or broth, and vinegar. Stir constantly.

● After approx. 20 minutes, add peeled, grated apple to cabbage. Stir and simmer for 40 to 50 minutes until cabbage is tender. Check often to make sure that there is sufficient liquid in the pot.

● Sprinkle with flour. Stir in cooked, peeled and chopped chestnuts. Add red wine to taste. Bring to a boil again and serve hot.

Potato Salad / Erdäpfelsalat

1 lb waxy potatoes	½ cup beef broth
2 oz lean Tyrolean bacon	salt
1 medium onion	black pepper
2 - 3 T oil	1 pinch sugar
1 ½ T wine vinegar	1 tsp capers, 2 tomatoes
1 T brown mustard	1 - 2 T chopped chives

● In a large pot, boil unpeeled potatoes until tender. Drain, let cool somewhat, and peel while potatoes are still warm. Slice and place in large salad bowl.

● Finely dice bacon. Peel and finely chop onion.

● Slowly heat oil in a medium pan and sauté onion and bacon. Douse with vinegar and pour over potatoes.

● Heat meat broth and stir in mustard. Add to potatoes. Season well and stir. Let stand at least 1 hour. Stir again and sprinkle with freshly chopped chives. Garnish with tomato wedges.

Green Beans with Bacon /
Fisolen mit Speck

1 ½ lbs green beans, salt	salt
3 T soft butter	pepper
1 onion, chopped	several cloves of garlic, if desired
10 thin slices of smoked bacon	beef broth

● Rinse green beans. If desired, cut ends and remove strings. Cook for approx. 20 minutes in boiling, salted water. Drain and briefly dip into very cold water to retain bright green color. Let excess water drip off.

● Butter a large casserole dish and sprinkle with chopped onion.

● Preheat oven to 350° F. Place strips of bacon on work surface and roll up bunches of beans. Arrange rolls in casserole dish, dot with butter and season. If desired, add cloves of garlic. Add beef broth.

● Bake for 15 - 20 minutes until done.

Our tip:
You can serve green beans wrapped in bacon with any meat or egg dish. They also go well with potato and rice dishes. You can also serve the beans with browned bread crumbs. Brown 4 T bread crumbs in 5 - 6 T butter.

Hot Beet Salad / Warmer Rohnen Salat

4 large, boiled potatoes	salt, pepper, dash of nutmeg
2 onions	1 pinch of sugar
2 T butter or shortening	1 - 2 T vinegar
1 boiled beet	2 T butter
6 T boiled green beans	

● Cut potatoes into fine slices. Brown with chopped onions in butter or shortening. Grate beet into potatoes. Add green beans and season. Add sugar. Sprinkle with vinegar and let cool.

● Place in a ceramic bowl and garnish with browned onions. Serve lukewarm.

Our tip:
You can serve Hot Beet Salad as a hot appetizer or as an accompaniment to meat dishes.

Cabbage with Bacon / Speckkraut

¾ lb Tyrolean bacon	1 small bay leaf
2 lbs sauerkraut	4 - 5 crushed juniper berries
salt, ground caraway, pepper	water or beef broth
	garlic to taste

● Dice bacon and brown in a large pot.

● Add sauerkraut, season, and cook over high heat for approx. 10 minutes, stirring constantly. Add water or broth and simmer about 30 minutes until tender.

● If desired, freshly crushed garlic can be added to taste.

Tyrolean Semolina Pudding / Bauernmus Tiroler Art

1 ½ T butter for skillet	4 cups milk
1 ¼ cups flour	4 cups water
salt	¼ cup melted butter
¾ cup semolina	cinnamon to taste

● Butter a large skillet. Combine flour and semolina in a separate bowl. Stir in half the water to form a thick batter. Add remaining water and milk to skillet and bring to a boil. Slowly stir in flour / semolina mixture. Reduce heat and allow pudding to thicken, stirring constantly. Remove from heat and let cool somewhat. Before serving, drizzle with melted butter. If desired, sprinkle with cinnamon. Serve warm.

F.Y.I.

Tyrolean Semolina Pudding, also called "Muas," "Muis," is often called a "Koch". It is a mainstay of the Tyrolean farmer's diet. Formerly, it was often served for breakfast to provide nourishment for a hard day's work. Nowadays, it is more commonly served as the evening meal.

Variations:
Cherry Pudding / Blueberry Pudding
Add 1 lb of fresh, pitted cherries to the "Muas" to make Cherry Pudding. Blueberry Pudding is made in a similar fashion. Wash and clean blueberries. Mix with sugar, lemon juice and cinnamon to taste before adding blueberries to the pudding.

Corn Meal Grits / Polenta

6 cups water	2 cups corn meal
salt	5 - 6 T butter
1 T butter	

● Bring water, salt, and 1 T butter to a boil. Slowly sprinkle in corn meal, stirring constantly as the mixture comes to a boil. After about 5 minutes, reduce heat and let simmer until corn meal mixture releases easily from spoon. Stir frequently. - Total cooking time: between 30 and 40 minutes.

● Turn mass out onto a cutting board and let cool. Roll out (about ½ inch thick) and cut into squares.

● Fry in a skillet with a generous amount of butter.

Fried Potatoes / Erdäpfelriebler

1 ½ lbs potatoes	flour
2 - 3 egg yolks	2 - 3 T butter
salt	

● Cook unpeeled potatoes until tender. Rinse under cold water and peel while still warm. Rice potatoes. When cooled, mix in beaten egg yolks and salt.

● Using a fork, cut in flour gradually until dough forms small flakes or balls.

● Melt butter in a large skillet and fry dough until golden brown, turning occasionally.

Skillet Corn Meal / Türkenriebler

1 ¼ cups corn meal	¼ cup butter or shortening
1 cup water	2 apples to taste
salt	

● Place corn meal in a large bowl and cover with boiling, salted water. Let stand at least 1 hour, stirring occasionally. This allows the corn meal to swell and soften.

● Melt butter or shortening in a large skillet. Add dough. Spread well in pan and let cook. If desired, you can also add thin slices of apple and stir with dough while cooking.

F.Y.I.
The breaking apart of the corn meal in the hot skillet is called "a'g'riblt" in Tyrolean dialect. Thus, the name "Riebler."

Cornmeal Hush Puppies / Maisriebler

2 cups milk	¾ cup corn meal
salt	approx. 2 T butter for frying
¼ cup butter	

● Bring milk to a boil. Stir in butter and salt. Gradually add corn meal, stirring constantly. Cook until corn meal no longer sticks to the side of the pan.

● Melt remaining butter in large skillet and spoon in corn meal dough.

● Continue frying, turning frequently.

Our tip:
You can either add diced, browned onion and bacon to the "Riebler" or, if preferred, serve with powdered sugar and fruit compote.

Tyrolean Egg Pancake / Eierschmarrn

¾ cup raisins
2 - 3 T rum
1 cup flour, salt
1 T powdered sugar
1 T vanilla sugar or 1 tsp vanilla extract
grated rind of ½ lemon
3 egg yolks
½ cup milk
3 egg whites
2 T powdered sugar
dash of lemon juice
5 T butter for frying
powdered sugar to sprinkle on top

● Rinse raisins briefly with boiling water, drain, and place in a bowl. Drizzle with rum and let stand.

● Sift flour into a mixing bowl. Add salt, powdered sugar, vanilla, grated lemon rind, egg yolks, and milk. Stir. Batter will be quite liquid. Let stand for approx. 30 minutes.

● Beat egg whites, powdered sugar and a few drops of lemon juice until whites form peaks. Gently fold egg whites into batter.

● Heat butter in large skillet. Add batter and spread raisins on top. Cover. Brown one side and then turn. Tear pancake

into pieces with two forks and continue frying until done.

Serve sprinkled with powdered sugar.

Our tip:
Cranberries, applesauce or fruit compote are good accompaniments for the Tyrolean Pancake.

Cheese Dumplings / Kasknödel

10 oz stale white bread	salt, nutmeg
4 eggs	½ cup butter
½ cup milk	5 oz cheese (Emmentaler)
1 onion	⅓ - ½ cup flour

● Cut bread into thin slices. Beat eggs and milk and pour over bread. Sauté finely chopped onions in butter until translucent. Finely dice cheese. Add onions, cheese and flour to bread mixture. Mix well, adding salt and nutmeg to taste.

● Form 8 - 10 dumplings from dough. Drop into boiling, salted water, reduce heat once water starts boiling again. Continue simmering approx. 15 minutes until dumplings are done.

Spinach Dumplings / Spinatknödel

10 oz stale white bread	salt, pepper, nutmeg
1 cup warm milk	2 T flour, 2 oz Tyrolean bacon, 2 eggs
1 ½ lbs pre-cooked, chopped spinach	1 - 2 T bread crumbs
1 clove garlic, crushed	3 T grated parmesan cheese
5 T butter, 1 small onion	

● Cut bread into thin slices. Pour warm milk over bread. Season spinach with garlic. Sauté finely chopped onion in butter, add spinach and simmer for approx. 5 minutes. Add flour and bread crumbs to bread / milk mixture. Then combine with beaten eggs, spinach and finely diced bacon. Mix well.

● Form 10 - 12 small dumplings from dough. Place in salted water which has been heated to a rolling boil. Reduce heat and let dumplings cook 15 - 20 minutes over a low flame until done.

● Drain dumplings. Place on platter, drizzle with brown butter and sprinkle with grated Parmesan cheese.
Serve immediately.

Tyrolean Semolina Dumplings / Tiroler Grießknödel

1 cup milk	1 stale hard roll, diced
3 T butter	1 ½ T butter, 2 eggs
1 cup semolina	1 T chopped parsley
2 oz Tyrolean bacon, diced	salt, pepper, nutmeg

● In a large pot, bring milk, butter and salt to a boil. Slowly sprinkle in semolina, stirring constantly until dough no longer sticks to side of pot. Let cool.

● Brown bacon and bread cubes in a large skillet, adding some butter.

● Beat eggs. Combine with chopped parsley and seasonings. Add to semolina, along with bread/bacon mixture. Stir well and let stand for several minutes.

● With wet hands, form dumplings. Drop into boiling, salted water. Cook for 10 - 15 minutes over a low flame until done.

Tyrolean Bacon Dumplings / Tiroler Speckknödel

1 onion	approx. 2 T flour
1 ½ T butter	1 T butter
3 - 4 stale hard rolls or Kaiser rolls	1 T chopped parsley
	1 T chopped chives
3 oz lean Tyrolean bacon, finely diced	salt
	pepper
3 eggs	marjoram
½ cup warm milk	

● Peel and finely dice onion, sauté in butter until translucent. Cut stale rolls into cubes, place in mixing

bowl with onions. Finely dice bacon and add to bread cubes.

● Mix eggs with milk and add to bread/bacon mixture. Add flour, butter, parsley, chives and seasonings and mix well. Let stand approx. 20 min.

● Meanwhile, fill a large pot with water and heat to boiling. Using wet hands form 8 dumplings. Gently place dumplings in water and immediately turn heat down to a gentle simmer. Let simmer for 10 - 15 min., drain and serve.

F.Y.I.

Tyrolean Bacon Dumplings are a mainstay of everyday Tyrolean food. There are many different recipes, but the basic elements are bread, bacon or ham. During Lent these dumplings are often made without bacon or ham and are browned in butter before boiling. Such dumplings are known as "Tiroler Fastenknödel" (Tyrolean Lenten Dumplings) and are served with sauerkraut.

Wine Noodles / Weinnudeln

2 cups milk, salt	wine sauce:
2 T butter	½ cup water, ¼ cup sugar
1½ T sugar	grated rind of ½ lemon
1 cup semolina, 2 eggs	1 whole clove
bread crumbs	½ stick cinnamon
6 T butter or shortening	1 cup dry red wine

● Bring milk and salt to a boil. Add butter and sugar, stirring well. Slowly sprinkle in semolina, stir constantly and cook until thickened. Let stand and cool.

● For wine sauce: Bring water and sugar to a boil. Add spices and red wine. Heat and then strain.

● On a wet cutting board, shape dough into a long roll. Cut into equal pieces and roll into finger-sized smaller rolls ("Nudeln"). Dip each "noodle" into beaten egg and then in bread crumbs. Brown in skillet with melted butter.

● Place finished "noodles" in a bowl. When all noodles have been browned, pour wine sauce over them and serve immediately.

Tyrolean "Home-Made Noodles" / Tiroler Hausnudeln

3 ½ cups flour	approx. 1 cup water
2 eggs, salt	7 T butter

● Form a smooth dough with sifted flour, eggs, salt, and water. Knead and then let stand at least 20 minutes.

● Cover work surface with flour and spread dough out very thinly. Sprinkle top of dough with flour. Roll dough up and cut into narrow strips. Let dry somewhat.

● In the meantime, bring salted water to a boil. Add noodles and let cook for about 10 minutes. Drain and rinse quickly with cold water. Serve with melted butter.

Spinach Gnocchi / Spinatnocken

1 ½ lbs spinach, 1 onion	approx. 1 ¼ cups bread crumbs
⅓ - ½ cup flour, 3 oz bacon	3 - 5 T milk, 3 eggs
1 ½ - 2 T butter	salt, pepper, nutmeg

● Remove stems, clean and cook spinach until tender. Put through a food mill. Finely chop onion and sauté in butter. Add spinach and stir well. Set aside to cool.

● Combine flour, bread crumbs, milk, eggs, and seasonings. Stir in spinach mixture. If dough is too thin, add more flour or bread crumbs.

● Dice bacon and brown in large skillet.

● Bring large pot of salted water to a boil. Use 2 tablespoons dipped in hot water to form dumplings. Water should no longer be boiling. Let dumplings simmer for approx. 20 minutes. Gently transfer to a colander to drain. Serve sprinkled with crispy bacon.

Tyrolean Cheese Spaetzle / Tiroler Kasspatzeln

2 ½ cups flour	1 T chopped parsley
2 eggs, salt	pepper
approx. 1 cup water	4 oz grated cheese (aged Emmentaler or Gruyère)
1 onion, 3 T butter	

● Quickly combine flour, eggs and salt with water to make batter. It should drop from the spoon in thick clumps.

● Bring pot of salted water to a boil. Holding a colander over the pot, press batter through holes to let droplets fall into hot water.

● Let simmer for 2 -3 minutes until all spaetzle come to the surface. Drain and rinse with cold water.

● Sauté finely chopped onions in butter. Add spaetzle and finely chopped parsley. Fry, turning frequently. Serve sprinkled with grated cheese.

Sweet Cheese Gnocchi / Süße Topfennocken

6 T butter	1 cup semolina
2 T sugar	3 T raisins
3 eggs, salt	salt
16 oz baker's cheese, well drained	6 T bread crumbs
	6 T butter

● Beat butter, sugar, eggs, and salt until creamy. Stir in baker's cheese, semolina and raisins. Let stand about 30 minutes.

● Bring salted water to a boil. Using 2 tablespoons dipped in hot water, form dumplings and drop into water. Allow to simmer for

10 - 15 minutes. Gently
transfer to a colander to
drain, and arrange on
plates. In a skillet, brown

bread crumbs in butter.
Spread over dumplings.
Serve with cherry
compote.

Potato Fritters / Erdäpfelblattln

¾ lb potatoes	1 ¼ cups flour
¼ cup butter	salt
1 egg	shortening for deep frying

● Boil unpeeled potatoes until tender. Drain and peel while still warm. Rice.

● Melt butter. Blend butter, egg, flour, and salt with potatoes.

● On a floured work surface, shape dough into a roll. Divide roll into several pieces. Roll each piece out until about ½ inch thick. Cut into 4-inch squares.

● Deep fry squares until golden brown.

Alpbach Honey Noodles / Alpbacher "Steffelnidai"

1 ¾ lbs potatoes	Honey sauce:
2 cups flour	flour, ¼ cup butter, 1 cup milk,
1 - 2 eggs	honey
salt, nutmeg	

● Boil unpeeled potatoes until tender. Drain and peel while still warm. Rice and knead quickly with flour, egg, salt, and nutmeg to form a smooth dough. Place dough on floured surface and roll out. Cut into small 1-inch squares. Fry squares in hot butter, place in a bowl and cover with honey sauce.

To make honey sauce: Brown flour in melted butter. Add milk and bring to a boil. Sweeten with honey.

F.Y.I.

These noodles are particularly popular on St. Stephen's Day (December 26). In the Alpbach Valley, they are therefore called "Steffelnidai" (St. Stephen's Noodles).

Tyrolean Bread Pudding / Scheiterhaufen Tiroler Art

5 stale rolls	grated rind of ½ lemon
2 cups lukewarm milk	¼ cup raisins
soft butter to grease form	¼ cup chopped almonds
¼ cup soft butter	1 lb apples
⅓ cup sugar	4 egg whites
2 T rum	2 T butter for dotting pudding
4 egg yolks	

● Cut rolls into thin slices, place in mixing bowl, cover with milk, and let stand for approx. 30 minutes, stirring occasionally. Preheat oven to 400° F.

● Butter a large casserole dish. Beat together butter, sugar, rum, and egg yolks. Combine with bread/milk mixture, raisins and almonds.

Peel apples. Cut into quarters, remove core, and cut into thin slices. Add to bread mixture. Beat egg whites until stiff peaks

form, and gently fold into mixture. Place mixture in buttered casserole, dot with butter and bake for 40 - 50 minutes until golden brown.

Our tip:
Instead of apples, you can use any other fruit. Rhubarb and cherries are particularly well suited. You can also use roasted hazelnuts (filberts) instead of chopped almonds.

Currant Fritters / Jochalstern

6 stale rolls, sliced (or white bread, cut into thirds)	Batter: 1 ½ cups flour
currant jam	1 cup milk
oil for deep frying	2 eggs, salt

● Spread jam on slices of rolls or bread. Form sandwiches.

● For the batter, combine flour with milk, eggs and salt.

● Heat oil in a large skillet or deep-fryer.

● Dip "sandwiches" into batter and then place in deep-fryer. Sandwiches can be placed close enough to touch one another in the fat. Turn as soon as they are somewhat browned on one side. Brown well on both sides. Serve hot.

Tyrolean Ruffles / Strauben

1 cup milk	1 T rum or brandy
pinch of salt	shortening for deep-frying
1 ¾ cups flour	powdered sugar
2 eggs	

● Bring milk to a boil. Add salt and sifted flour. Let cool somewhat, stirring occasionally.

● Add egg yolks and rum or brandy. Stir. Beat egg whites until they form stiff peaks, and gently fold into milk mixture.

● Place batter in a pastry

bag and "spritz" dough in circular fashion into hot fat. Let brown on all sides.

Serve hot "Strauben" sprinkled with powdered sugar.

F.Y.I.

In Tyrol, "Strauben" are primarily eaten as popular holiday specialties. They can be made of a variety of batters. In the above recipe, it's important that the batter is smooth and flows easily. Strauben can also be made of a milk-cream puff batter. In any case, they are sprinkled with lots of powdered sugar and served hot. One generally drinks a hearty elderberry wine or simply a strong cup of coffee with "Strauben." If they are served as a main dish, Strauben are usually served with a fruit compote or applesauce.

Grape Strudel / Traubenstrudel

Dough:

2 cups flour

1 egg

1 - 2 T oil, salt

¼ - ⅓ cup water

Filling:

2 lbs grapes

⅔ cup sugar

grated rind of ½ lemon

1 tsp cinnamon

¾ cup bread crumbs

¼ cup melted butter

powdered sugar

● Sift flour into a large bowl. Make a well and drop in egg, oil and salt. Knead into a smooth dough, gradually adding just enough water to form a semi-firm dough. Knead by hand until dough has a silky appearance. Cover and let rest for 30 minutes.

● For the filling: Clean and wash grapes. Let drip dry. Mix sugar, grated lemon peel and cinnamon.

● Cover large table with tablecloth or clean sheet. Sprinkle with flour. Roll out dough as thinly as possible. Then, using the backs of your hands and knuckles, stretch dough outward from the center until it is almost transparent. Cut off thicker edges of the dough. Sprinkle dough with bread crumbs. Distribute grapes over dough and sprinkle with sugar / cinnamon mixture.

● Preheat oven to 375° F.

● Fold sides of dough in over grapes. Gently use cloth to help roll dough into a strudel. Transfer strudel to greased cookie sheet. Baste with melted butter.

● Bake for 40 - 50 minutes, basting occasionally with melted butter. Remove from oven and sprinkle with powdered sugar.

Tyrolean Peasant Cookies / Tiroler Bauernlaibl

²/₃ cup sugar	1 ¹/₃ cups flour
2 eggs	20 - 25 whole almonds, shelled

● Mix eggs and sugar until creamy. Add sifted flour gradually until a smooth, soft dough is formed.

● Using 2 teaspoons, drop dough approx. 1 inch apart onto a cookie sheet that has been greased or lined with baking paper.

● Place whole almond in the center of each dough drop. Bake in preheated oven at 290° F for approx. 15 minutes or until golden brown.

● Makes approx. 25

Anise Cookies/ Anislaibl

4 eggs	butter for greasing pan
1 ¾ cups powdered sugar	1 tsp ground anise
2 ½ cups flour	

● Butter and flour cookie sheet. Tap off excess flour. Preheat oven to 290° F.

● In a deep mixing bowl, beat eggs and powdered sugar until very foamy. Add ground anise and mix briefly.

● Gradually add just enough sifted flour to make a smooth, yet light, dough.

● Using 2 teaspoons, drop dough approx. 1 inch apart onto cookie sheet.

● Bake for approx. 15 minutes until golden brown. Makes about 40 cookies.

● Makes approx. 40

Almond Cookies / Muskazonerl

²/₃ cup sugar	2 T bread crumbs (moisten with rum)
2 egg yolks	1 - 2 T rum
1 tsp lemon juice	
¾ cup ground almonds	

● In a deep mixing bowl, beat eggs and sugar until very foamy.

● Add lemon juice, ground almonds and rum-moistened bread crumbs. Blend well.

● Preheat oven to 300° F. Line cookie sheet with baking paper or parchment. Drop batter in spoonfuls about 1 inch apart. Bake for 15 - 20 minutes.

● Makes approx. 20 - 25

Tyrolean Doughnuts / Ziachkiachl

3 ¾ cups flour	3 egg yolks
1 ¼ oz yeast	½ cup melted butter
¼ cup sugar	½ tsp salt
approx. 1 cup lukewarm milk	oil for deep-frying

● Sift flour into a deep mixing bowl. Form a well and fill with crumbled yeast, some milk and sugar. Stir and let rest in a warm spot for approx. 30 minutes. Then add remaining milk, egg yolks, butter, and salt. Mix to form a smooth dough which pulls easily away from sides of bowl.

Let rise at least another 15 minutes.

● Sprinkle work surface with flour and form a roll of dough. Cut into equal pieces. Roll pieces into balls. Let rise.

● Heat deep-fryer.

● Using both hands, pull dough apart in the middle

until almost transparent, leaving a thick border (see picture). Deep-fry until edge of fritter is golden brown and center is still light, turning only once.

Our tip:

According to Tyrolean tradition, "Ziachkiachl" are either served filled with marmalade or with a fruit compote.

Fig.:
"Ziachkiachl" and "Brandstrauben"

55

Sweet Buns / Wuchteln

3 ¾ cups flour, salt	1 tsp vanilla extract
1 ¼ oz yeast	6 T softened butter
approx. ¼ cup lukewarm milk	grated rind of ½ lemon
1 egg	½ cup butter for basting
⅓ cup sugar	apricot marmalade or prune filling

● Sift flour into a deep mixing bowl. Form a well and fill with crumbled yeast, some milk and some sugar. Stir and let rest in a warm spot for 20 - 30 minutes. Then add remaining milk and sugar, vanilla, egg, butter, and grated lemon peel. Mix to form a smooth dough which releases easily from sides of bowl.

● Sprinkle work surface with flour and roll dough out about 1-inch thick. Cut into squares. Put a teaspoon of apricot marmalade or prune filling in the center of each square and close dough around filling.

● Butter a large pan or casserole and place filled dough squares with smooth side up and touching one another in the pan. Cover and let rise 15 - 20 minutes. In the meantime, preheat oven to 375° F.

● Generously baste tops of dumplings with butter. Bake for about 45 minutes. Baste again with butter. Dumplings are done when golden brown.

Our tip:
"Wuchteln" are wonderful with <u>vanilla sauce</u>. To make sauce, bring 2 cups milk, pinch of salt and a vanilla bean to a boil. In another saucepan, whip 2 egg yolks with ⅓ cup sugar until very light in color. Then add 2 T cornstarch and beat until smooth. Gradually add milk mixture to egg/sugar/

starch mixture and bring to a gentle boil. Remove vanilla bean and let sauce cool somewhat, stirring occasionally. You can also add ¼ cup whipping cream if you like a richer sauce.

Tyrolean Christmas Fruit Bread / Tiroler Weihnachtszelten

For most Tyrolean farming families, as well as many other Tyrolean households, baking a Christmas "Zelten" is part of the Advent preparations. Since this fruit bread needs to stand for some time, many communities bake their "Zelten" on St. Thomas'

Day (November 28). Because this fruit bread is so rich and its composition indicated the prosperity of the household, many of the ingredients were prepared well ahead of time. Dried pears, dried plums, dried figs, as well as plump raisins must be chopped finely. Hazelnuts, almonds and pine nuts need to be shelled, and together with the candied lemon and orange peel finely chopped. Only then is the dough prepared, or in some regions made by local bakers. As a final touch, typical spices like anise, caraway, coriander, cinnamon, ground cloves, as well as a dash of brandy are added.

When cool, the loaves are stored in a cool place.

Of the many variations throughout Tyrol, the following recipe is a particularly traditional one:

½ lb prunes	2 tsp ground cinnamon
½ lb dried pears	juice and grated rind of 2 oranges
1 lb dried figs	
1 lb large raisins	4 - 6 T brandy or rum
5 - 6 cups water	2 - 3 T lemon juice
½ lb hazelnuts	2 lbs dark bread dough or bread dough made of 2 lbs rye flour
2 lbs almonds	
3 ½ oz pine nuts	
¼ lb candied orange peel	1 ¼ oz yeast, some sugar
¼ lb candied lemon peel	approx. 1 cup lukewarm water
¾ cup sugar	
½ tsp each ground cloves, ground anise and salt	salt
	butter for cookie sheet
	sugar water for basting

- Rinse prunes, pears, figs, and raisins in cold water. Place in bowl, cover with water, and let stand overnight.

- Drain softened fruit and dice. Finely chop hazelnuts, almonds and pine nuts. Add nuts to candied orange peel, candied lemon peel, sugar, cinnamon, spices, salt, orange juice and grated orange rind, as well as brandy or rum and lemon juice, and combine well with dried fruits. Let stand.

- Prepare bread dough. Place rye flour in large mixing bowl. Make a well in center of flour, crumble in yeast and mix with some sugar and water. Cover dough and let stand for 30 minutes in a warm spot. Then add remaining water and salt. Knead well. Let stand again for 30 - 40 minutes.

- Add fruit mixture to bread dough and mix very well. Form rectangular or round loaves ("Zelten") and place these on a buttered cookie sheet. Let rise. Preheat oven to 400° F.

- Bake loaves for 60 - 75 minutes, basting often with sugar water. Remove when golden brown. Remove immediately from baking sheet and let cool.

Pine Nut Crescents / Pignolikipferl

1 ¼ cups ground almonds	1 tsp vanilla extract
1 ½ cups sugar	grated rind of 1 lemon
4 egg whites	approx. 8 oz whole pine nuts
²/₃ cup finely chopped raisins	

● Beat egg whites until stiff. Combine with ground almonds, sugar, vanilla, and grated lemon rind.

● In a large skillet over low flame, heat batter until a soft, malleable mass forms. Then add raisins and stir.

● Form 2 long rolls of dough and let cool in refrigerator for about 30 minutes.

● Cut rolls into ½-inch slices. Form finger-sized rolls, bend into crescents. Sprinkle with pine nuts.

● Place crescents on greased cookie sheet and bake at 375° F for 15 - 20 minutes.

Upper Inn Valley Gingerbread / Oberinntaler Lebkuchen

²/₃ cup sugar	2 tsp cinnamon
2 eggs	¹/₈ tsp ground cloves
4 oz honey	dash of ground nutmeg
¾ cup ground hazelnuts	grated rind of ½ lemon
1 ½ oz candied orange rinds	2 level tsp baking powder
	1 ¾ cups flour

● Beat eggs and sugar until creamy. Stir in honey and ground nuts. Then add finely chopped candied orange rinds, cinnamon, remaining spices, and grated lemon rind.

● Sift together flour and baking powder. Gradually add to honey mixture and combine well.

● Let stand for at least 1 hour.

● On a floured work surface, knead dough well.

Roll until about ½ inch thick. Using a cookie cutter or knife, cut dough into circles or squares. Place on well-greased cookie sheet and bake for 20 - 25 minutes in a 360° F oven.

Our tip:

Use almond halves to garnish gingerbread circles or squares. Brush cookies with beaten egg prior to baking and then decorate with almonds.

Chocolate Cherry Cake / Dunkler Kirschkuchen

½ cup softened butter	¾ cup grated baking chocolate
½ cup sugar	
1 tsp vanilla extract	1 tsp unsweetened cocoa powder
1 pinch of salt	
5 egg yolks	5 egg whites
½ cup ground almonds	½ cup sugar
6 T milk	¾ lb pitted cherries
1 ¾ cups flour	butter and bread crumbs for cake pan
2 tsp baking powder	
	powdered sugar

● Grease and coat 12-inch round cake pan with bread crumbs. Preheat oven to 360° F.

● Add to softened butter, one after another, sugar, vanilla, salt, and egg yolks. Beat until very creamy. Add ground almonds and milk. Using a sifter, add flour and baking powder to batter, stirring constantly. Mix in grated chocolate and cocoa powder.

● Beat egg whites until slightly stiff. Gradually add sugar and continue beating until it forms stiff peaks. Mix 3 tablespoons of egg whites into batter, and then fold in remainder.

● Pour batter into prepared cake form immediately. Smooth surface and distribute cherries evenly on top.

● Bake for 50 - 65 minutes. Let cool in pan before removing, sprinkle with powdered sugar.

Our tip:
Serve your Chocolate Cherry Cake with a traditional specialty, "Maibutter" (sweet whipped cream). To make this, beat 1 cup whipping cream with ¼ cup sugar until stiff. Sprinkle with cinnamon and serve.

Innsbruck Pound Cake / Innsbrucker Kuchen

- Rinse raisins under hot water, let drip. Pat dry with paper towel, place in bowl and drizzle with rum. Let stand about 1 hour.

- Finely chop candied citrus rinds.

- Beat butter and sugar

until very light in color. Add eggs one by one, beating constantly. Mix in vanilla, grated lemon rind and rum, the latter drop for drop.

- Sift flour, baking powder and salt together. Add to batter along with raisins and chopped citrus rinds,

| ¼ cup light-colored raisins |
| 1 T rum |
| ¼ cup (2 oz) candied lemon peel |
| ¼ cup (2 oz) candied orange peel |
| ¾ cup butter |
| ¾ cup sugar |
| 6 eggs |
| 2 tsp vanilla extract |
| grated rind of ½ lemon |
| 3 T rum |
| 2 tsp baking powder |
| 2 ½ cups flour, pinch of salt |
| butter and bread crumbs for cake pan |

tirring to make a smooth
atter.

Butter and line a 12-inch
af pan with bread crumbs.
our in batter and bake for
0 - 60 minutes at 360° F.

Our tip:
When cooled well and
wrapped in aluminum foil,
Innsbruck Pound Cake
stays fresh for days.

Tyrolean Nut-Fruit Stollen / Tiroler Nuß-Früchte Stollen

Dough:	
3 ¾ cups (1 lb) flour	2 oz hazelnuts
2 cakes compressed yeast (1 ⅓ oz)	2 oz dried apricots
⅔ cup sugar	2 oz chopped candied lemon rind
approx. ½ cup lukewarm milk	½ cup (4 oz) marzipan
1 egg	½ cup sweet cream
¾ cup soft butter	Baste with: 6 T melted butter
Filling: 2 oz chopped pistachio nuts	Sprinkle with: powdered sugar

● For the dough: Sift flour into a deep mixing bowl. Make a well in the middle, crumble in yeast and stir in half the sugar and milk. Cover and let "sponge" stand in a warm spot for 15 - 20 minutes.

● Add remaining milk and sugar, as well as the egg and butter. Knead to a smooth dough, namely until it loosens easily from edge of bowl and forms bubbles. Cover and let stand for about 30 minutes.

● In the meantime, prepare filling: Coarsely chop pistachios and hazelnuts. Finely dice dried apricots and candied lemon peel. Combine these with pieces of marzipan and cream. Knead well.

● Place risen dough on a floured surface and roll out into a rectangle. Spread filling onto dough. Fold dough in toward center along both long sides to form the typical "stollen" shape (see photo). Preheat oven to 360° F.

● Place stollen on well-greased cookie sheet and let rise another 15 minutes. Bake for 45 - 55 minutes.

● Once cooled, sprinkle stollen generously with powdered sugar.

Poppyseed Kugelhopf / Mohnguglhupf

● Butter and sprinkle fluted tube pan with bread crumbs. Preheat oven to 360° F.

● In the following order, beat together butter with sugar, salt, vanilla extract and eggs until very light

¾ cup + 2 T soft butter
¾ cup sugar, pinch of salt
2 tsp vanilla extract
4 eggs
2 ½ cups flour
½ cup cornstarch
1 T baking powder
3 T rum
approx. ½ cup milk
¼ cup (2 oz) ground almonds
¾ cup (6 oz) ground poppy seeds
powdered sugar
butter and bread crumbs for cake pan

and creamy. Sift together flour, cornstarch and baking powder and add to batter. Mix well. Then add rum, milk, ground almonds, and ground poppy seeds. Pour batter into fluted

pan and bake for 60 - 70 minutes.

● Let cool slightly in pan. Turn pan over and let cool completely. Sprinkle with powdered sugar.

Hall Tartlets /
Haller Törtln

Almond dough:
⅔ cup ground almonds

¾ cup powdered sugar

cinnamon, ground cloves

1 egg

Tartlet batter:
4 egg yolks

¾ cup + 2 T sugar

¾ cup ground almonds

1 oz candied orange peel

1 oz candied lemon peel

cinnamon, cardamom,
ground cloves

4 egg whites

baking parchment, cut into
3-inch circles

Glaze:
1 ¼ cups powdered sugar

1 egg white

1 - 2 T hot water

● First mix almond dough by combining ground almonds, sifted powdered sugar, egg, cinnamon, and ground cloves to form a smooth dough. Set aside.

● In a second bowl, beat egg yolks with sugar until light and creamy. Stir in ground almonds, finely chopped candied lemon and orange peel, and spices. Beat egg whites until stiff and fold into batter.

● Preheat oven to 275° F. Place parchment circles on baking sheet.

● With a pastry bag, first spritz almond dough around the edge of the parchment circles. Then fill center of circles with tartlet batter. Bake for 30 - 40 minutes.

● To make glaze, combine egg white, sifted powdered sugar and hot water. Drizzle over cooled tartlets.

● Makes approx. 30

Our tip:
If you prefer, you can use lemon juice or strained fresh orange juice instead of hot water for the glaze.

Bread Baking

Bread is one of the major cornerstones of the Tyrolean diet. Bread-baking is therefore steeped in tradition. Even though the variety of breads commercially available has grown over the years, baking bread oneself nevertheless provides an economical and tasty way to augment any meal.

In Tyrol, wheat, rye and combinations of these grains are most popular. Wheat and rye flour are particularly good to bake with. Yeast or sourdough starter serves as leavening. The most commonly used spices are salt, caraway, fennel, and diverse seeds.

It is essential that the dough be given adequate time to rise and that it is well kneaded. Below you will find the most important bread-baking tips.

Flour

Whole-grain flours made of wheat or rye should always be used immediately after grinding, as the flour loses its flavor and aroma the longer it is exposed to air.

Water / Liquid

Regardless of the liquid used (water or buttermilk), the following always holds true:

● The liquid should be **lukewarm** (best temperature around 95° F). Always add gradually to dough. The amount of liquid used depends on how much the flour will absorb. Pre-ground flour always requires **less** liquid; freshly ground flour may need **more**.

● The **dough** must not be too soft, but instead should be elastic and **firm**. It should not stick.

Leavening

● Yeast is generally used for breads made of wheat flour, and

● sourdough has proven

itself for rye breads.

It is also possible to use a combination of yeast and buttermilk, or yeast and sourdough starter, when

baking mixed-grain breads.
Always use fresh yeast,
which should smell a bit like
wine. Dry yeast should be
used only when it is

specifically made for bread
baking.

Tips for Baking Bread and Preparing Dough

● Your kitchen should be warm and free of drafts.

● All ingredients should be at room temperature. Liquids should be lukewarm (about 95° F).

● Do not use metal bowls if making sourdough bread. Plastic, glass or ceramic bowls are better.

● When adding liquids to the dough, do so gradually. The dough must be elastic and firm.

● Bread dough must be well kneaded. We recommend using a stand mixer for heavy doughs. Doughs should be kneaded until they lift away from the bottom of the bowl.

● Doughs containing a higher percentage of rye flour tend to stick. Therefore, wait about 10 minutes after adding liquid to let flour expand before handling dough. Then knead until dough is smooth.

● Allow adequate time for bread dough to rise properly. For breads made of wheat flour, standard times suffice. Breads made with sourdough may need up to 60 minutes to rise adequately. The times given in the recipes are therefore only guidelines.

● Wheat breads made with yeast should be baked at a constant temperature. Rye or mixed breads with sourdough are best baked at dropping temperatures (preheat oven to 400° F, then lower heat to bake at 350° F).

● Bread is done when it sounds hollow when tapped on the bottom, or when the inside temperature reaches 200° F.

● Always let bread cool on a wire rack to allow moisture to evaporate.

Rustic Peasant Bread / Rustikales Bauernbrot

1 ¼ cups coarsely milled rye flour	salt, pepper, caraway, fennel, coriander
2 ¼ cups finely ground rye flour	up to 3 cups lukewarm water
2 ¾ cups wheat flour	¾ cup sourdough starter
3 ½ cups coarsely ground wheat flour	2 compressed ⅔-oz yeast cakes
3 T sunflower seeds (shelled)	additional rye flour, oil for baking sheet

● Mix different kinds of flour, sunflower seeds and spices in a large mixing bowl. Make a well in the middle. Crumble yeast into the well and add a little water to start dissolving the yeast.

● Add sourdough starter and very gradually add remaining water, kneading to make a smooth dough. A stand mixer with dough hooks works nicely.

● Continue kneading by hand. Shape into ball.

● Cover and let stand in a warm location for at least 20 - 30 minutes. Preheat oven to 425° F.

● Oil baking sheet and sprinkle with flour. Knead dough again and form a round loaf. Place loaf on baking sheet.

● Make a design on the top of the loaf with a fork or sharp knife.

● Baste with water and place in hot oven. Reduce heat to 375° F after 15 - 20 minutes.

● Bread should bake for a total of 60 - 75 minutes.

Our tip:
Instead of sunflower seeds, you can also use hulled pumpkin seeds.

Four-Grain Bread/
Vierkornbrot

2 cups rye flour

3 ¾ cups all-purpose flour

2 compressed ⅔-oz yeast cakes

2 T honey

approx. 1 cup lukewarm water

approx. 1 cup lukewarm buttermilk

2 -3 T flax seeds

2 -3 T sunflower seeds

1 - 2 T pumpkin seeds

½ - 1 T salt, pepper

1 T bread spice mixture

● Combine different kinds of flour in a large mixing bowl. Make a well in flour, crumble yeast into well. Add honey and lukewarm water. Mix to form a thick sponge.

● Cover and let rest in a warm location for 20 - 25 minutes. Then add all remaining ingredients one at a time. Mix well, using a stand mixer with dough hooks. Knead well by hand and place in a

well-greased large loaf pan. Cover and let rise for another 20 - 30 minutes. Preheat oven to 375° F.

● Pierce top of risen dough with a fork several times and place in hot oven.

● Bake for 50 - 60 minutes.

Pretzels / Fastenbrezeln

1 lb whole wheat flour	3 cakes compressed yeast
1 lb all-purpose flour	1 ½ oz baking soda, water
2 ¼ - 2 ¾ cups lukewarm water	coarse pretzel salt
2 T salt	oil for baking sheet

● Combine two types of flour in large mixing bowl. Dissolve yeast in a little water, then add to flour along with remaining water. Mix well and knead vigorously. We recommend using a stand mixer with dough hooks.

● Once dough is smooth, divide into golf-ball sized pieces. Roll these out until they are about 12 inches long, tapering toward ends to leave middle of roll somewhat thicker. Shape pretzels and place on flour-coated baking sheet. Let rise 30 - 40 minutes.

● In a ceramic bowl mix baking soda and 1 qt warm water to make a 5% solution. Dip each pretzel in solution and place on a well-greased, lightly floured baking sheet.

● Preheat oven to 420° F. Bake pretzels for 15 - 25 minutes. If desired, sprinkle pretzels with coarse salt before placing in oven. Serve fresh out of the oven.

Bacon-Onion Bread

2 lbs all-purpose flour	5 oz smoked, lean Tyrolean bacon
2 cakes compressed yeast	
approx. 3 cups lukewarm water	1 large onion
	butter or oil for baking sheet
1 tsp salt, pepper	

● Dice bacon and brown in large skillet until crispy. In the meantime, peel and finely chop onion. Add to bacon and sauté until translucent. Remove from heat and let cool.

● For the yeast dough, sift flour into a large mixing bowl. Make a well in the middle, crumble yeast into well, add some water, and mix into a thick sponge.

● Cover and let rest in a warm location for 20 - 30 minutes.

● Dissolve salt in remaining, lukewarm water. Alternatively add some of bacon-onion mixture and water to dough while kneading well, until ingredients are gone. Knead well. We recommend using a stand mixer with dough hooks.

● Form a round loaf. Place on well-greased baking sheet and let rise another 15 - 20 minutes.

● In the meantime, preheat oven to 375° F. Pierce upper surface of loaf with a fork. Bake for 45 - 60 minutes.

About the Recipes:

Oven temperatures are given for ovens with top and bottom heat. If you prefer to use a convection oven, reduce heat by about 50° F. Baking times generally remain the same.

Guide to Abbreviations:

I have used the following abbreviations or terms in this book:

lb(s)	pound(s)
min	minute(s)
oz	ounce(s)
T	tablespoon
tsp	teaspoon(s)

Photo credits:

Fotostudio Teubner, Füssen: Front cover, p. 25, 27, 39, 47, 61
Austrian Tourism Promotion, Vienna: Back cover, p. 1, 2, 5
Günther Haas, Innsbruck: p. 3
Bosch Appliances Ltd., Munich: p. 16, 64, 67, 68, 72, 77
Komplettbüro GmbH, Munich: p. 23, 31
Siggloch Edition, Künzelsau: p. 12, 43

"Landesausschuss" of the Autonomous Province of Bolzano: p. 8, 40, 41
Upper Austrian Power Plants AG Photo Archives, Linz: p. 14, 51
Salzburg State Office of Tourism: p. 19, 20
Langnese-Iglo GmbH, Hamburg: p. 29
Fotostudio Sattelberger, Munich: p. 45, 55, 58
Knorr-Maizena, Heilbronn: p. 57
Vitri, Mühltal: p. 33

The author and publisher would like to thank the above organizations for providing an excellent selection of photographic material.
English translation by:
Mary Heaney MARGREITER

© **KOMPASS-Karten GmbH**
   Rum/Innsbruck
Fax 0043(0)512/265561-8
e-mail: kompass@kompass.at
http://www.kompass.at
First Edition 2000

Publication No.: 1719
ISBN 3-85491-167-X